MW01355692

1ST
UP

THE GIRL WHO PICKED UP BUT NEVER PUT DOWN

Written and Illustrated by
Madison Girifalco

Dedicated to my
Grandma Cathy and Grandpa Louis

The girl who picked up but never put down
lived two blocks away from the far side of town.

She liked her friends

So she took off her crown,
the last thing to put down,
and enjoyed her treasures
with everyone around.

The king of the clutter, she thought with a smile,
"You can't be a king, if you don't have a pile."

It was hard to admit, but she had to confess,
as she gave away more, she wanted less.
She emptied her arms till she had shed
every treasure but the crown on her head.

Piece by piece, the weight started to fade
and she watched with pride at the joy she had made.

So she went on her way giving gifts down the block,
"Have a flip flop, a flower, have this glittery rock!"

so she handed it over and suddenly such
a weight had been lifted, her friend's face was bright.
"Hey, putting down is kind of alright."

“Wow what a pile, can I help you with that?
I especially like your taxidermy cat.”
The cat was her favorite... but it was a bit much,

She tried to play too, but the pile was heavy.
She couldn't tumble or hop and still hold it steady.

It wobbled and tipped and blocked out the sun
and all of her friends began to run.

All of them except for one...

MAIL

The monkey bars, the chalk, the tall drinking fountain...
They even shared laughter playing king of the mountain.

they were sharing!

K+L

"The treasures, the gadgets, they're all mine!" she uttered,
as she picked up a crown: The King of the Clutter.

But every good king needs plenty of praise
so she left for the playground to impress and amaze
the kids who had gawked at her pile before
because then it was good, but now she had more!

"Look at all I've collected!" she announced with pride,
then waited a moment for cheers to subside.
But the cheers never started, not a person was caring.
She peaked over her pile and saw...

The girl had collected so much that her pile
had grown to the sky -- up nearly a mile!

Red woolen socks and a snake's old skin
A boxed Jack that popped out but wouldn't go in
Boas and bass drums and bluish green bottles
Joke books and fish hooks and aeroplane models...

she kept on collecting
and look what she got...

She went on like this without much of a thought
excited at having what others did not

4:28
2:32

A man on the street only asked for the time
from one of her watches -- after all, she had nine!
How awkward, she thought, but then she declared it,
"I would if I could, but I just cannot spare it."

Sam and his friend asked if she would mind
sparing a sticker, “the shiny pink kind”

“If I give you a sticker, then he’ll want one too.
Once everyone wants one, what will I do?”

But there were still people that gathered in packs,
hoping to lighten the load off her back.

these things she picked up, but wouldn't put down
'cause she might have to share if she left them around.

But what she liked best was picking stuff up!
From feathers, to buttons, to old polished spoons,
to tall wooden masks that looked like baboons,

and hugging her pup...

Originally from Wilmington, Delaware, Madison moved to Los Angeles to pursue writing. Her work is a reflection of strong convictions, an active imagination, and determination to challenge her readers' habits and perspectives. When not writing or illustrating, she spends her time building puppets, advocating for social justice, and growing food in her garden.

www.mindovermadison.com

Special thanks to Ma, Pop, and Louis for the love and support,
I couldn't be luckier.

Made in the USA
San Bernardino, CA
23 May 2018